be green.

Don't be blue. Be green.
How to help to save our planet.

by Monica Sheehan

RUNNING PRESS
PHILADELPHIA · LONDON

9   8   7   6   5   4   3   2
Digit on the right indicates the number of this printing

Library of Congress Control Number: 2006930239
ISBN: 978-0-7624-3232-5

Conceived, written, and illustrated by Monica Sheehan.
Produced exclusively for Running Press Book Publishers by:
Herter Studio
432 Elizabeth Street
San Francisco, CA

This book may be ordered by mail from the publisher.
Please include $2.50 for postage and handling.

But try your bookstore first!

Running Press Book Publishers
2300 Chestnut Street
Philadelphia, PA 19103-4371

Visit us on the web!
www.runningpress.com

be green.

Don't be blue. Be green.
How to help to save our planet.

For Michael and Stephen Kroon

Special thanks to Leigh Grahill, Michael Kroon,
Benson Chiles, Carol Davies, Traci Sheehan,
Tina Klem, Chris Clarity, and to my sister Nora

THE EARTH DOES NOT
BELONG TO MAN,
MAN BELONGS TO THE EARTH.
ALL THINGS ARE CONNECTED...
MAN DID NOT WEAVE
THE WEB OF LIFE,
HE IS MERELY A STRAND IN IT.
WHATEVER HE DOES
TO THE WEB,
HE DOES TO HIMSELF.

CHIEF SEATTLE 1854

be green.

Things have changed...

the world isn't
what it used to be

and the news isn't good.

Our planet is in trouble...

and we're running out
of time.

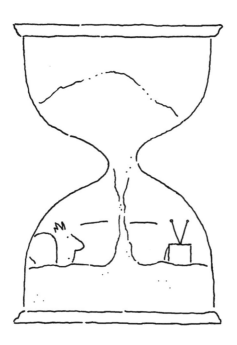

Everything we love
on this earth is at stake,
If we continue to
ignore the warnings.

We can no longer tell ourselves
that "they" will
solve the problem.

There is no they.
We are the they.
The decision is ours.

Are we going to just
sit by and watch
the destruction
of our Mother Earth
and her future
for our children?

(Your heart will tell you what to do.)

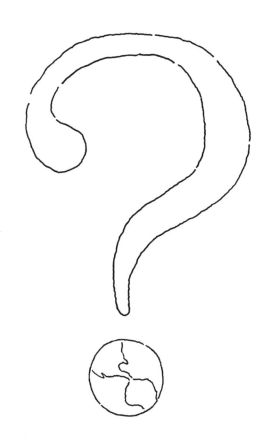

We must rise to the occasion

and answer the Call.

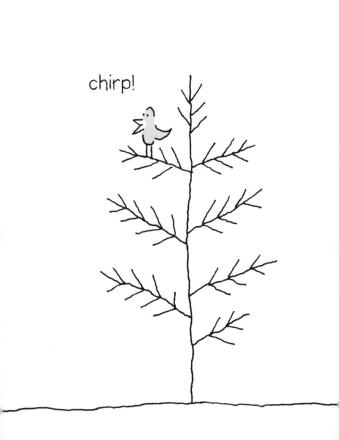

But first we must face the truth

Our continued dependence on and building
of carbon-spewing coal-burning plants

and our gas-guzzling nation
are causing irreparable damage.

There are too many, using too much

Our lands and forests are disappearing.

Our oceans are suffering,
Arctic glaciers are melting,
species are vanishing...

But don't be blue...

be green.

(green means go!)

Just take the first step.

start.

MAKE A PLEDGE
to protect our planet
and to help
stop global warming.

COMMIT to being part of
this exciting time
of positive change,
to get creative,
to re-invent,
to fight the good fight,
and to act now!

Say no to traffic jams
junk
pot bellies
mass consumption
over spending
debt
BIG OIL!

NO

YES

Say yes to saving money
being healthier
being happier
having a more meaningful life
saving the planet
and having fun!
(what a deal!)

Educate yourself. CO Who?

Carbon Dioxide (CO_2) is the main cause of global warming, released into the air when we burn fossil fuels like oil (gas) and coal (electricity).

Since fossil fuels are our primary energy source, every time you turn on the car, tv, or light, you begin emitting CO_2.

THE US IS ONLY 4% OF THE WORLD'S POPULATION YET CONTRIBUTES 25% OF CO2 EMMISIONS. —NRDC

Global Warming

As greenhouse gases (mainly CO2)
increase more of the sun's heat
is trapped. Hence, global warming.

Conserve water.

THIRTY-SIX STATES ARE ANTICIPATING WATER SHORTAGES BY 2016. YET THE AVERAGE AMERICAN USES MORE THAN 100 GALLONS OF WATER EACH DAY.
-EPA

A FAMILY OF FOUR USING LOW-FLOW SHOWERHEADS INSTEAD OF FULL-FLOW MODELS CAN SAVE ABOUT 20,000 GALLONS OF WATER PER YEAR.
-NRDC

40% OF THE DRINKING WATER SUPPLIED TO HOMES IS FLUSHED DOWN THE TOILET.
-THE GREEN BOOK

● Get low-flow
shower heads
faucets, & toilets.

● Turn off the water
while you're brushing
your teeth.

● ...and fix
those leaks!

Flip the switch
(when you leave the room
for more than 15 minutes).

Flip.

Flip.

Flip.

click.

Kill your energy vampires.

UNPLUGGING YOUR VAMPIRES CAN SAVE AS MUCH AS 40% OF THE WASTED ELECTRICITY.
–THE GREEN MACHINE

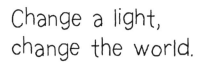

Change a light,
change the world.

IF EVERY U.S.
HOUSEHOLD REPLACED ITS
MOST COMMONLY USED
INCANDESCENT BULBS WITH
COMPACT FLUORESCENTS, WE'D CUT
OUR ELECTRICITY USE FOR LIGHTING
IN HALF—AND LOWER OUR ANNUAL
CO_2 EMISSIONS BY ABOUT
62.5 MILLION TONS
—SIERRA CLUB

R-E-C-Y-C-L-E.
Show me you can save a tree.

bottles and cans
clap your hands!

There's no
reason not to-

Cause save Mother Earth
You know, we got to.

DON'T FORGET ABOUT CELLPHONES, COMPUTERS, AND
OTHER HOUSEHOLD ITEMS. GO TO EARTH911.ORG AND ENTER
YOUR ZIP CODE TO FIND OUT WHAT AND WHERE TO RECYCLE.

DRINK TAP
and refill your water bottle.

SAVE THE ENVIRONMENT (AND LOTS OF MONEY) BY USING A FILTER ON YOUR FAUCET TO FILL UP REUSABLE BOTTLES. AMERICANS GO THROUGH AN INCREDIBLE 2.5 MILLION PLASTIC BOTTLES EVERY HOUR, AND MOST ARE NOT RECYCLED. FURTHERMORE, PLASTICS ARE MADE FROM A MIX OF PETROLEUM AND CHEMICALS THAT CAN TRANSFER INTO THE WATER. (WE LIKE SIGG OR KLEAN KANTEEN WATER BOTTLES),

–i GOGREEN

Don't leave a legacy
of styrofoam.

25 BILLION STYROFOAM CUPS ARE THROWN AWAY EACH YEAR. THE US MAKES ALMOST THREE MILLION TONS OF IT (STYROFOAM) EACH YEAR, THE MAJORITY OF WHICH GOES TO LANDFILLS.

-THE LIVE EARTH GLOBAL WARMING SURVIVAL HANDBOOK

P.S. bring your own mug to work.

IN THE U.S. ALONE, WE THROW AWAY 100 BILLION PLASTIC BAGS EACH YEAR—THE EQUIVALENT OF 12 MILLION BARRELS OF OIL. YIKES!
—SIERRA CLUB

Just say no (thank you) to plastic bags!! and bring your own.

Conservation begins at home.
Save energy. Save money.
Save the environment.

START WITH
CAULKING AND WEATHER-
STRIPPING ON DOORWAYS AND
WINDOWS. THEN ADJUST YOUR
THERMOSTAT AND START SAVING.
FOR EACH DEGREE YOU LOWER
YOUR THERMOSTAT IN THE
WINTER, YOU CAN CUT YOUR
ENERGY BILLS BY
3 PERCENT.

FINALLY,
ASK YOUR UTILITY
COMPANY TO DO A
FREE ENERGY AUDIT OF
YOUR HOME TO SHOW
YOU HOW TO SAVE
EVEN MORE MONEY.
-SIERRA CLUB

Put a blanket on your water heater and set the thermostat no higher than 120F.

A WATER HEATER BLANKET COULD SAVE 1,000 LBS. OF CARBON AND $40 PER YEAR (AND THEY'RE ONLY $15!). SETTING YOUR THERMOSTAT SAVES 550 LBS. OF CARBON DIOXIDE AND $30 PER YEAR.
–STOPGLOBAL WARMING.ORG

Wash your clothes in cold or warm water (not hot), and hang up a clothes line.

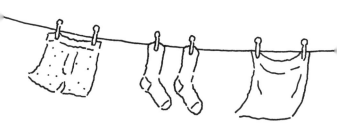

Tune Your Ride.

NO SUV

Change your air filter.

Inflate your tires.

Call your utility company and switch to green power.

RENEWABLE ENERGY SOLUTIONS,
SUCH AS WIND AND SOLAR POWER, CAN
REDUCE OUR RELIANCE ON COAL-BURNING POWER
PLANTS, THE LARGEST SOURCE OF GLOBAL WARMING
POLLUTION IN THE UNITED STATES. CALL YOUR LOCAL
UTILITY AND SIGN UP FOR RENEWABLE
ENERGY. IF THEY DON'T OFFER IT,
ASK THEM WHY NOT?
-SIERRA CLUB

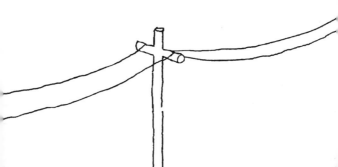

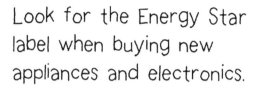

Look for the Energy Star
label when buying new
appliances and electronics.

BY CHOOSING ENERGY-STAR QUALIFIED PRODUCTS
CONSUMERS CAN CUT THEIR ENERGY BILLS BY 30%,
SAVING ABOUT $400 DOLLARS PER YEAR. -ENERGY STAR

Get black-listed from junk mail.

WITH 17.8 TONS
OF JUNK MAIL DELIVERED
ANNUALLY BY EACH OF THE
U.S. POSTAL SERVICE'S 293,000
LETTER CARRIERS, THE AVERAGE
AMERICAN SPENDS 8 MONTHS OPEN-
ING BULK MAIL OVER THE COURSE
OF HIS OR HER LIFE AND STILL
ENDS UP THROWING 44% OF
IT AWAY UNOPENED!
- iGO GREEN

GO TO
41LBS.ORG TO
GET BLACK-LISTED
OR JUST CALL THE
COMPANY AND ASK
TO BE TAKEN OFF
THEIR LIST.

Stop the paper chase.
Over 1/3 of all waste is paper.

PAY YOUR BILLS ONLINE AND SEND E-VITES.

THE LOSS OF OUR TREES NOT ONLY LEADS TO ANIMALS LOSING THEIR HABITATS AND BECOMING EXTINCT, BUT CONTRIBUTES DIRECTLY TO GLOBAL WARMING. DEFORESTATION ACCOUNTS FOR UP TO 25% OF THE CARBON EMISSIONS THAT LEAD TO CLIMATE CHANGE. OUR TREES ARE MOTHER NATURE'S LUNGS! ONE WAY TO SAVE THEM IS TO GO PAPERLESS.
—THINKMTV.COM

THE AVERAGE U.S. OFFICE WORKER GOES THROUGH 10,000 SHEETS OF PAPER A YEAR. SO START RECYCLING IT!

Reduce your garbage.

THE AVERAGE
AMERICAN GENERATES
4.5 POUNDS OF TRASH
EVERY DAY, WHICH IS ALMOST
TWICE THE AMOUNT OF TRASH
THE AVERAGE AMERICAN
PRODUCED DAILY IN 1960.

-ENERGY INFORMATION
ADMINISTRATION

BUY IN
BULK. BUY
MINIMALLY
PACKAGED
GOODS.

TRY
COMPOSTING,
AND REDUCE YOUR
HOUSEHOLD GARBAGE
BY ALMOST 500lbs.
PER YEAR.
-ENERGY INFORMATION
ADMINISTRATION

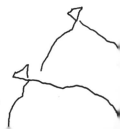

Go public. Use public transportation

or carpool one or more times a week.

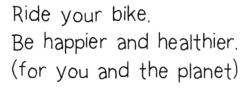

Ride your bike.
Be happier and healthier.
(for you and the planet)

IN COPENHAGEN
33% OF COMMUTERS
TRAVEL BY BIKE. PERHAPS
IT IS NO COINCIDENCE THAT
A RECENT SURVEY RANKED
DENMARK AS THE HAPPIEST
OF 178 COUNTRIES.
–GLOBAL WARMING
SURVIVAL HANDBOOK

BE AN
INSPIRATION
FOR HOW THE
WORLD CAN BE.
RIDE YOUR
BIKE.

Just walk...

to the store

to work

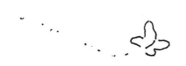

Get a push mower
and keep your lawn
pesticide-free.

Food travels on average over 1,500 to 2,000 miles. Food for thought. Buy local/in season/organic.

Eat less meat.
(Beans, it's what's for dinner.)

ACCORDING TO A 2006 UN REPORT, THE LIVESTOCK SECTOR IS ONE OF THE TOP TWO OR THREE MOST SIGNIFICANT CONTRIBUTORS TO GLOBAL WARMING. IT SPEWS MORE GREEN HOUSE GAS INTO THE ATMOSPHERE THAN THE ENTIRE TRANSPORTATION SECTOR.
—ENVIRONMENTAL DEFENSE

IF EVERY AMERICAN HAD ONE MEAT-FREE DAY PER WEEK IT WOULD BE THE SAME AS TAKING 8 MILLION CARS OFF US ROADS.
—ENVIRONMENTAL DEFENSE

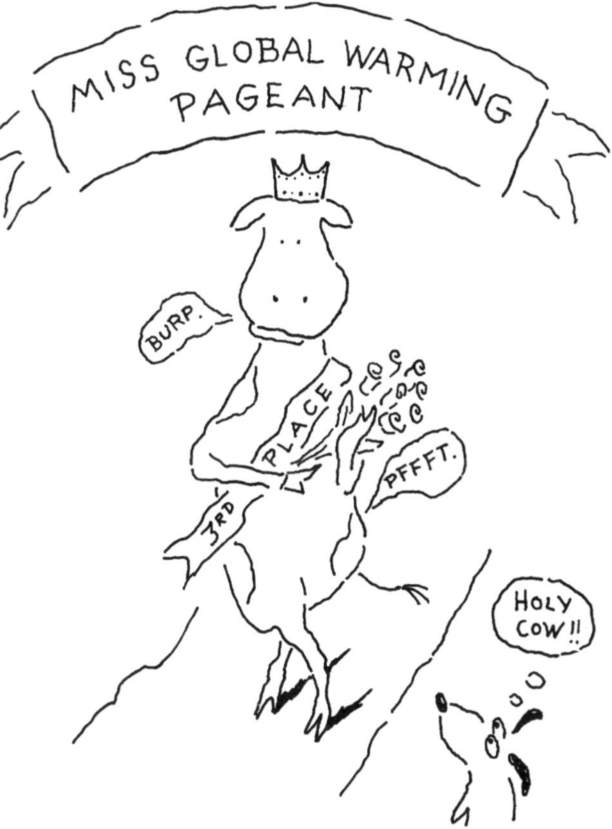
MISS GLOBAL WARMING
PAGEANT
BURP.
3RD
PLACE
PFFFT.
HOLY
COW!!

Buy a Fuel-Efficient Car.
It's one of the most important things you can do (1/3 of CO_2 is from transportation).
So buy a Hybrid! Or go biodiesel

FUEL ECONOMY
PEAKED IN 1987 AND
HAS ESSENTIALLY BEEN
DECLINING SINCE THEN DUE
TO OUTDATED STANDARDS
AND INCREASED SALES OF
FUEL-WASTING SUVS AND
OTHER LIGHT TRUCKS.
-NRDC

THE AVERAGE
DRIVER COULD SAVE
16,000 LBS. OF CO_2
AND $3,750 PER YEAR
DRIVING A HYBRID.
-STOPGLOBAL
WARMING.ORG

Very cool.

So NOT Cool.

Shop green.

BUY
ECO-FRIENDLY
CLEANING PRODUCTS.
FEWER CHEMICALS MEAN
FEWER POLLUTANTS
GETTING INTO OUR
AIR, LAND, AND
WATERS.

BUY
RECYCLED
PRODUCTS LIKE
TOILET PAPER,
PAPER TOWELS
AND NAPKINS.

VOTE FOR
MOTHER EARTH
WITH YOUR POCKETBOOK.
SUPPORT COMPANIES THAT
ARE GREEN AND DON'T
SUPPORT THOSE THAT
AREN'T. (AND GET
A GREEN OR CLIMATE
CREDIT CARD!)

Plant a Tree
and join others in preserving
and protecting the forests.

A SINGLE TREE WILL ABSORB ONE TON OF CO2 OVER ITS LIFETIME,
MAKING CLEAN AIR FOR US TO BREATHE. TREES ALSO PROVIDE
SHADE THAT CAN REDUCE YOUR AIR CONDITIONING BILL BY 10 TO 15%.

Be a green light for others!
Put a windmill in your backyard.
Go solar. Go geothermal.

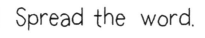

Spread the word.

Tell your Mayor.
Tell your mother.

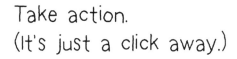

Take action.
(It's just a click away.)

CONTACT YOUR
REPRESENTATIVE
ABOUT REDUCING OUR
DEPENDENCE ON COAL
AND OIL. GO TO
WWW.HOUSE.GOV./WRITEREP/
TO FIND YOUR
REPRESENTATIVE'S
WEBFORM ONLINE.

JOIN ONE OF
THE ENVIRONMENTAL
ORGANIZATIONS THAT ARE
TAKING POLITICAL ACTION.
ENVIRONMENTAL DEFENSE AND
THE SIERRA CLUB WILL EMAIL
YOU PETITIONS TO SIGN
AND THE INITIATIVES
TO SUPPORT

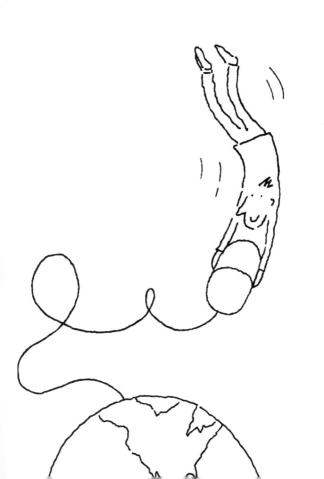

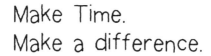

Make Time.
Make a difference.

FORM A GREEN
ACTION COMMITTEE
TO HELP MAKE YOUR
TOWN, SCHOOL, OR
WORKPLACE GO GREEN. GO TO
COOLCITIES.US (TOWN) OR
11THHOURACTION.COM
(SCHOOL/BUSINESS) TO
HELP GET YOU
STARTED.

GET
INVOLVED WITH
ORGANIZATIONS
THAT ARE
MAKING A
DIFFERENCE.

Vote for Mother Earth.
Vote for our children's future.
Vote for green candidates!

MOST OF THE TECHNOLOGY AND ALTERNATIVES ALREADY
EXIST AND WE MUST DEMAND FROM OUT POLITICAL LEADERS
THAT THEY BE INTEGRATED INTO POLICY. —11TH HOUR ACTION

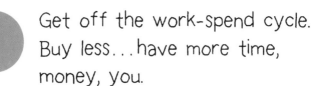

Get off the work-spend cycle.
Buy less... have more time,
money, you.

The best things in life are flea.
Think vintage. Think antique.
Think second-hand.

KEEP PERFECTLY GOOD STUFF OUT OF LANDFILLS.
CHECK OUT FREECYCLE, SWAP, AND CRAIG'S LIST.
P.S. HAVE A CLOTHES SWAP PARTY WITH YOUR FRIENDS!

So live simply...share...

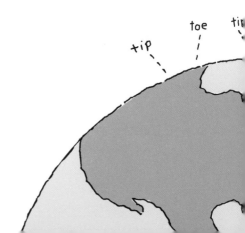

and tread lightly on the planet.

Fall in love with nature...

so you'll want to protect her.

And realize
that every action
you take...

has power.

Because if you do it...

and she does it...

and he does it...

and they do it...

We can...

Be the change.

I Pledge to

- [ ] Be part of the generation that did SOMETHING, (and not part of one that did nothing) in the face of global warming.

- [ ] Recycle (no cheating!).

- [ ] Ride my bike, walk, or take public transportation at least once a week.

- [ ] Write a letter to my congressman.

- [ ] Join an environmental organization.

- [ ] Think twice, and consider the earth's life in my lifestyle.

- [ ] Reduce my own carbon footprint.

- [ ] Sign the International 7 Point Pledge. (ipledge-climateprotect.org)

Organizations to join

The Sierra Club-www.sierraclub.org
America's oldest, largest, and most influencial
grassroots environmental organization. Works
to protect wild places and the planet.

NRDC (National Resources Defense Council)
www.nrdc.org-Non profit that uses law, science,
and the support of its members to protect
the planet for all living things.

Environmental Defense
www.environmentaldefense.org.-Partners
with businesses, governments, and communities
to find practical environmental solutions.

The Alliance for Climate Protection
www.climateprotect.org-Persuading Americans and
the rest of the world of the urgency in adopting
effective solutions for the climate crisis.

Stop Global Warming-www.stopglobalwarming.org
A collective encouraging governments, corporations,

and politicians take the steps to stop global warming.

11th Hour Action-www.11thhouraction.com
Action site for Leonardo DiCaprio's film The 11th Hour. A hub of information for individuals and communities to take action and share information on environmental issues.

some cool sites on the web

think.mtv.com -Break the Addiction
A 12-month action plan to fight global warming and the effects of over-consumption.

iGOGREEN www.ivillage.com/green
A site for women encompassing organic food, and eco-friendly fashion and decor. Sign up for emailed tips and facts about living green.

www.carbonfund.org
Reduce what you can. Offset what you can't. Learn about and buy carbon offsets.

www.bikeleague.org- Working to improve the quality of bicycling in America. Learn about lobbying for bike paths.

www.computertakeback.com/.-Find a responsible recycler for your old computer (and help reduce the more than 2.5 million tons of electronic waste that is dumped into landfills each year).

www.localharvest.org-A website to find farmers' markets, family farms, and other sources of sustainably grown food in your area.

www.freecycle.org-A nonprofit movement of people who are giving (& getting) stuff for free in their own towns. It's about reuse and keeping good stuff out of landfills.

www.mysigg.com-Sigg Kanteen Safe, refillable water bottles online

www.wholefoodsmarket.com-Whole Foods Market The world's largest retailer of natural and organic products, with stores throughout North America.

We love this earth as
a newborn loves its mother's
heartbeat. Love it as we
have loved it. Care for it,
as we have cared for it.
Hold in your mind the memory
of the land as you receive it.
Preserve the land
for all children,
and love it, as God loves us.

CHIEF SEATTLE 1859